Birds
and
Other Things in Nature

by Gloria Gentile

DORRANCE
PUBLISHING CO
EST. 1920
PITTSBURGH, PENNSYLVANIA 15238

Dorrance Publishing Co
585 Alpha Drive
Suite 103
Pittsburgh, PA 15238
Visit our website at *www.dorrancebookstore.com*

ISBN: 978-1-4809-5539-4
eISBN: 978-1-4809-5562-2

Acknowledgments

Stokes, Donald and Lillian, Bird Behavior

Staff

Susan Peverelle

Wood Duck

Wood Duck

1. Wood ducks live in holes in trees and nest boxes.

2. They build their nests from March until June.

3. They may use woodpecker homes to build their nests.

4. They lay approximately fifteen eggs in one birth. If they lay more than fifteen eggs, an activity known as "egg dumping" is used. This is when wood ducks use the nests of other birds for their extra eggs.

Peregrine Falcon

1. The peregrine was on the decline because DDT was used as a pesticide.

2. Many people worked hard to establish their return.

3. Peregrines build their nests from February to March.

4. Peregrines are aggressive toward other falcons and turkey vultures.

5. The female is the dominant one of the pair.

6. The peregrine is a large, beautiful hawk.

Peregrine Falcon

Osprey

1. The osprey is the only hawk that dives into the water.

2. It lives near humans, so the osprey is an excellent hawk to observe.

3. The average nest size is six feet long and four feet deep.

4. The female is larger than the male. The female is twenty-three inches long.

Osprey

Pileated Woodpecker

1. The pileated woodpecker is the biggest woodpecker. It is twenty inches long.

2. In the northeast they are rare because the forests were cleared.

3. They are afraid of humans.

4. The pileated woodpecker requires 275 acres to build their nests. In this way, their hatchling birds are safe.

5. They have fights with snakes that climb trees and enter the hole and eat the eggs.

Pileated Woodpecker

Scarlet Tanager

1. The scarlet tanager is one of the most beautiful birds. (It is my favorite bird.)

2. The male is easy to spot. The female is harder because she is the same color as the leaves in which she nests.

3. One of the most interesting things about the male is that he molts to a yellow plumage from his natural red color.

4. The tanager builds her nest in May. The female does all the nest building.

5. The streaking of the hatchlings' plumage is different from the parents'.

Scarlet Tanager

Cardinal

1. The cardinal is the favorite bird of many people because of its beauty.

2. Mate-feeding is the highlight of the relationship between the male and female cardinals. The male brings food to the female, and they touch beaks as she accepts the food.

3. Courtship is from March to July.

4. The female builds her nest between April and July. She seeks the wild rosebush to place her nest.

5. They communicate with each other by singing. He starts the song and she answers by matching his song.

6. During the fall, he is very aggressive toward his mate. But when winter arrives, he is once again very tolerant of her.

Some Birdwatching Sites on or near Long Island

1. Jamaica Bay Preserves, Jamaica, NY

2. Jones Beach, Wantagh, NY

3. JFK Sanctuary, Wantagh, NY

4. Muttontown Preserve, East Norwich, NY

5. Shu Swamp, Mill Neck, NY

6. Beaver Dam, Locust Valley, NY

7. Audubon Sanctuary, Oyster Bay, NY

8. Caumsett, Huntington, NY

9. Target Rock, Huntington, NY

Other Things

Christmas sledding by the lake

Refreshment stand and Walkway at the Overlook. Captree State

Farm in Long Island

Rockport, Maine 1995

Great Locations

1. Rockport - a beautiful place. I was attending an art class in Maine, and one of the places to see was the lighthouse and the historical buildings that were adjacent to the lighthouse. It was a very beautiful sight.

2. Christmas 2001 - Upstate, New York. We came upon a beautiful lake, and there we saw a couple all bundled up on a beautiful sled drawn by a horse. We waved to them and they shouted, "Merry Christmas!"

3. Captree - Great park! My husband and I loved to crab and fish here. I remember that one day I took a hike around the bay, came back, and found my husband had twenty (yes, twenty) crabs in the pot. Yummy!

Scholastic Activites

Make Words From:

Independent -

_____
_____
_____
_____
_____

Vocabulary -

_____
_____
_____
_____
_____

Education -

_____
_____
_____
_____
_____

Ornithology -

_____
_____
_____
_____
_____

For example: Substantiate - sub, tan, ate, tent, bus, tease (you get the idea).

Draw a map of the United States.

Match the columns: North, South, East, West

a. Middle State   _____Massachusetts

b. Eastern State   _____Quebec

c. Southern State   _____Ottawa

d. St. Anne's de Bupre   _____Montana

e. Northern State   _____Texas

f. Vancouver, Canada   _____Kansas

g. Capital of Canada   _____Western region, Canada

The questions below have to do with the birds in this book.

1. What bird dives into the water to catch food?

2. What bird uses "egg dumping" when laying extra eggs?

3. What bird has a Sherlock-type cap?

4. What female bird is larger than her mate?

5. What bird uses woodpecker homes to build nests?

6. What bird almost disappeared because of a pesticide?

7. What bird uses 275 acres and fights off a snake when the snake tries to eat the bird's eggs?

Math Fun

How many birds are there?

A lake has twelve wood ducks, two pileated woodpeckers, and five peregrines. They fly over the lake and they wade in the water, but when winter comes some of the birds leave the lake. They are five wood ducks, two pileated woodpeckers, and two peregrines. Now how many birds are left at the lake?

Try this:

4x = 12   x=_____   7x = 847 x=_____

5x=100   x=_____   8x=336 x=_____

6x=426   x=_____   9x=0   x=_____